Got Have S'mores

Go Crackers with the Best 40 Campfire-free Recipes - So much S'more than just another Cookbook!

BY

Gordon Rock

Copyright 2018 Gordon Rock

License Notes

No part of this Book can be reproduced in any form or by any means including print, electronic, scanning or photocopying unless prior permission is granted by the author.

All ideas, suggestions and guidelines mentioned here are written for informative purposes. While the author has taken every possible step to ensure accuracy, all readers are advised to follow information at their own risk. The author cannot be held responsible for personal and/or commercial damages in case of misinterpreting and misunderstanding any part of this Book

Table of Contents

Introduction 6

Sweet Treats 8

    Campfire Muffins 9

    Caribbean-Style S'mores 11

    Dark Chocolate S'mores Pretzels 13

    Dipped Apple S'mores 15

    Double Chocolate S'mores Stuffed Cookies 17

    Florida Orange Chocolate Dipped S'mores 20

    Fully Loaded S'mores Popcorn 23

    Key Lime Pie S'mores 25

    Melting S'mores Toastie 27

    Minty S'mores 29

    PB&S Dip 30

    Peanut Butter and Apple S'mores Pizza 32

    Perfect Pudding 34

Raspberry and Apricot S'mores 36

Rose Mallow and Vanilla Wafer, White Chocolate S'mores . 38

Simple S'mores Ice Cream 40

S'mores Bark 42

S'mores Breakfast Oatmeal 44

S'mores Cheesecake 46

S'mores Fudge 50

S'mores Hand Pies 52

S'mores Hand Pies 54

S'mores on a Stick 56

S'mores Stuffed French Toast 58

S'mores Sushi 60

S'mores Toffee 63

Strawberry Skillet S'mores 65

Sunflower S'mores Dip 67

Tempting S'mores Truffles 69

The Original 71

White Chocolate and Raspberry S'mores 73

Drinks 75

Boozy S'mores Coffee 76

Champagne and Vodka Cocktail 78

Chocolate and Mallow S'mores Margarita 80

Flaming S'mores Vodka and Rum Cocktail 82

Hot Chocolate with Mallows and Crumbs 85

Irish Whiskey in the Jar 87

Oh So Sweet S'mores Smoothie 89

Party S'mores Jello Shots 91

S'morestini 93

S'mores Shake 96

About the author 98

Author's Afterthoughts 100

Introduction

S'mores are one of America's and Canada's favorite campfire snacks, but there is lots s'more we can tell you about these oeey gooey, melting treats.

Here are some fun foodie facts.

The graham cracker was first invented in 1829 by Sylvester Graham, a Presbyterian minister. He created it as a food to help control carnal urges!

Over 90,000,000 pounds of marshmallows are bought by Americans each year

The very first recipe for s'mores was published in 1927 not in a cookbook though but in the Girls Scouts handbook.

On August 10th every year the nation celebrates National S'mores Day

The first time the word s'mores became known was 44 years ago in 1974

The world's largest s'more was created by Pennsylvania where campers built a huge s'more weighing in at just under 270 pounds comprising of 140 pounds of marshmallows, and 90 pounds each of chocolate and graham crackers!

The Guinness World Record for the largest number of people making s'mores at any one time is 423. The record was set on April 21st in 2016, in California's Huntingdon Beach

The Girl Scouts re-introduced s'mores cookies to their 2018 cookie line-up

The Gotta Have S'mores Cookbook brings together 40 camp-fire free recipes for you snacking enjoyment!

Sweet Treats

Campfire Muffins

All the flavor of your favorite campfire treat in a soft and fluffy muffin. Enjoy warm while the mallows and chocolate are still melting and gooey.

Servings: 12

Total Time: 45mins

Ingredients:

- Butter (for greasing)
- ¼ cup granulated sugar
- 3 cups graham cracker crumbs
- 2 tsp baking powder
- 1 medium egg (beaten)
- 2 tbsp organic honey
- 1 cup whole milk
- 4 ounces semisweet choc chips
- 1½ whole graham crackers (broken into small pieces)
- ½ cup mini mallows

Directions:

1. Preheat the main oven to 350 degrees F. Grease a 12-hole muffin tin.

2. Add the sugar, graham cracker crumbs, and baking powder in a bowl and stir to combine.

3. Stir in the beaten egg, honey, and milk followed by half of the choc chips.

4. Spoon the batter into the muffin tin, filling the holes approximately ⅔ of the way.

5. Combine the remaining choc chips, broken graham crackers, and mini mallows in a small bowl and sprinkle evenly over the batter in the tin. Gently press any large pieces further down into the batter.

6. Place in the oven and bake for just over 20 minutes until golden. Allow to cool to warm before serving.

Caribbean-Style S'mores

Tangy pineapple is the perfect pairing with sweet marshmallows while graham cracker squares provide crunch and texture to this tasty treat.

Servings: 4

Total Time: 8mins

Ingredients:

- Butter (for greasing)
- 4 slices fresh pineapple (peeled, cored, cut into ½" thick rings)
- 8 large marshmallows
- 8 graham cracker squares

Directions:

1. Grease a pan and over moderately high heat, grill the pineapple for approximately 2 minutes each side, or until grill marks begin to form and the pineapple is warmed through.

2. Place 2 marshmallows on each cracker and microwave for 15-20 seconds, until the marshmallows expand a little.

3. Arrange a slice of pineapple on top of half of the toasted mallow topped crackers and sandwich with a second cracker, marshmallow side down.

Dark Chocolate S'mores Pretzels

Oeey gooey, sweet and salty – what more can anyone want from a simple snack?

Servings: 14 pretzels

Total Time: 40mins

Ingredients:

- ½ cup semi-sweet choc chips
- 2 tbsp whole milk
- 28 mini salted pretzels
- ⅓ cup graham crackers (crumbled)
- ½ cup mini mallows

Directions:

1. Melt the choc chips along with the milk in a small pan, while frequently stirring to ensure that the chocolate doesn't stick and burn the bottom of the pan. This will take around 2-3 minutes.

2. Carefully dip each pretzel into the melted mixture, gently shaking off any excess. Transfer to a wire baking rack.

3. Immediately dip the chocolate coated pretzels into the cracker crumbs, repeating the process until all 14 of the pretzels are coated.

4. Add 14 of the dipped pretzels to a baking sheet. Top the pretzels with approximately 3-4 mini mallows each and on high, place under a broiler to allow the mallows to brown. This will take between 1-2 minutes. Carefully watch the mallows to avoid them burning.

5. Top each of the 14 pretzels with another pretzel to form a sandwich.

6. Serve warm or transfer to the fridge, to chill.

Dipped Apple S'mores

Forget toffee apples; these s'mores dipped apples are way tastier!

Servings: 8

Total Time: 1hour 30mins

Ingredients:

- Nonstick spray
- 8 large Granny Smith apples (washed, dried, stems removed)
- 2 tbsp butter
- 2 (16 ounce) packs large marshmallows
- 2 cups graham crackers (coarsely crushed)
- 11½ ounces milk choc chips

Directions:

1. Line a cookie sheet with wax paper and generously coat with nonstick spray.

2. Insert popsicle sticks into each of the 8 apples

3. In a large pan, over moderate heat, melt the butter.

4. Add the marshmallows to the melted butter and stir to combine.

5. One at a time, dip the apples into the warm mallow mixture, allowing any excess mixture to drip off.

6. Transfer the apples to the cookie sheet and place in the fridge to set for 15 minutes.

7. Add the graham cracker crumbs to a shallow bowl.

8. In the top of a double boiler, melt the choc chips, stirring until silky.

9. Dip the bottom half of the apples into the melted chocolate and then into the cracker crumbs.

10. Place the dipped apples onto the cookie sheet and transfer to the fridge until set.

11. Enjoy.

Double Chocolate S'mores Stuffed Cookies

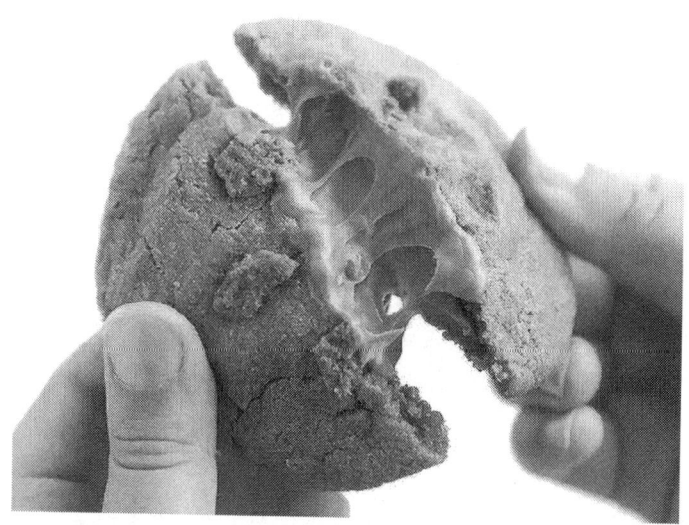

Soft and chewy cookies are studded with mallows and milk chocolate chunks and chips. Enjoy warm with a big ol' glass of milk.

Servings: 16

Total Time: 25mins

Ingredients:

- 1½ cups graham crackers (broken into small pieces)
- 1½ cups flour
- ¼ tsp baking powder
- ¼ tsp salt
- 8 ounces salted butter
- ¾ cup light brown sugar
- ¾ cup granulated sugar
- 2 eggs
- 1 tsp pure vanilla essence
- 1 cup milk choc chips
- 64 mini mallows
- Chunky chocolate (chopped into small bite-sized pieces)

Directions:

1. Preheat the main oven to 350 degrees F.

2. Combine the graham crackers, flour, baking powder, and salt in a bowl.

3. In a second bowl, cream together the salted butter, brown sugar, and white sugar. Beat in the eggs and vanilla essence.

4. Add the flour mixture to the butter/egg mixture, beating until combined.

5. Fold in the milk choc chips.

6. Roll the cookie dough into 2 ounce balls and place on baking sheet. Be sure to leave space between each cookie. Place in the oven and bake for several minutes.

7. Take out of the oven and press 4 mallows and 3 mini chocolate chunks, into each cookie.

8. Pop back in the oven for a few more minutes until the mini mallows are lightly browned.

9. Allow to cool and set up a little before enjoying.

Florida Orange Chocolate Dipped S'mores

Chocolate and orange, a winning combination! A sweet and satisfying snack, or dessert.

Servings: 6-8

Total Time: 2hours 30mins

Ingredients:

- 1 tbsp Florida orange zest
- 1 cup Graham crackers (crumbled)
- 1½ cups all-purpose flour
- ¼ tsp kosher salt
- ½ cup +1 tbsp Florida orange juice
- 1 packet dry yeast
- ⅓ cup honey
- 1 cup warm water
- ½ cup 55% cocoa chocolate
- ½ cup sugar
- 1 cup Florida tangerines (segmented)
- 8 large marshmallows

Directions:

1. Using an electric stand mixer, combine the orange zest with the crumbled crackers, all-purpose flour and kosher salt and on low speed.

2. In a mixing bowl, combine 1 tbsp of orange juice with the yeast, honey, and warm water.

3. Set the mixture aside to rest for a few minutes and add to the orange zest-cracker mixture, while increasing to a moderate speed. After approximately 5 minutes, set the dough aside to proof in a warm place.

4. As soon as the dough has doubled in size, after 40-45 minutes, punch it down, roll it into a suitably sized loaf pan, and let rise for an additional 15 minutes.

5. Bake at 325 degrees F for around 40 minutes.

6. While the bread bakes, melt the chocolate.

7. Dip the segments of tangerine halfway into the melted chocolate and place in the fridge to harden.

8. In a pot, melt the sugar. Pour in the ½ cup of orange juice and boil for 60 seconds, until reduced. Cook the liquid for a few more minutes and then drizzle it over the mallows.

9. As soon as the bread is sufficiently baked, set to one side to cool.

10. When cool, slice into ¼" thick pieces. Top each piece with a marshmallow and a dipped tangerine.

Fully Loaded S'mores Popcorn

Movie night just got better with this tasty sweet popcorn loaded with sticky marshmallows, melted choc chips, and crunchy graham cracker crumbs.

Servings: 6-8

Total Time: 45mins

Ingredients:

- 1 cup brown sugar
- 1 cup salted butter
- 16 ounces large marshmallows
- 16 cups plain popcorn
- ½ cup milk choc chips
- 1 cup graham cracker crumbs
- 1 cup mini mallows

Directions:

1. Line a baking sheet with parchment, set to one side.

2. Melt together the sugar and butter in a saucepan.

3. Add the regular mallows and continue to heat, while stirring, until they melt and combine with the butter.

4. Add the popcorn to a large bowl and pour over the butter/mallow mixture. Stir with a rubber spatula until the popcorn is coated evenly.

5. Sprinkle over the choc chips, cracker crumbs, and mini mallows stirring again until evenly distributed.

6. Transfer the popcorn to the baking sheet and set aside for half an hour to set.

Key Lime Pie S'mores

Our two favorite desserts come together to form the perfect marriage between zesty key lime pie and sticky s'mores.

Servings: 6

Total Time: 10mins

Ingredients:

- 6 large marshmallows
- ¾ cup Key lime pie filling or Key lime curd
- 6 whole graham crackers (snapped in half)

Directions:

1. Light a ring on your stove top.

2. Thread the marshmallows on skewers and hold just above the flame, turning as necessary so that they are evenly toasted.

3. Spread 2 tbsp of curd/pie filling on half of the graham crackers and top each with a melted marshmallow. Sandwich together with the remaining graham cracker halves and enjoy straight away.

Melting S'mores Toastie

Bring a smile to your face with each melt in the mouth bite of this simple yet delicious toasted sandwich.

Servings: 1

Total Time: 10mins

Ingredients:

- 3 tbsp marshmallow crème
- 2 slices whole grain bread
- 4 square chunks milk chocolate

Directions:

1. Preheat a panini press to moderately low heat.

2. Spread the marshmallow crème evenly onto one side of each slice of bread.

3. Place the chocolate on one of the slices and place the second slice on top (marshmallow side down).

4. Place on the press and heat for 5 minutes or until the filling is nicely melted.

5. Slice and enjoy straight away.

Minty S'mores

The perfect sweet treat to enjoy in the great outdoors made using just two ingredients. Cozy up around the campfire and get roasting!

Servings: 2

Total Time: 5mins

Ingredients:

- 2 large marshmallows
- 4 thin mint cookies

Directions:

1. Using kitchen scissors cut each marshmallow in half.

2. Roast the mallows over an open fire or flame.

3. Sandwich the mallows between 2 cookies and enjoy.

PB&S Dip

You've heard of PB&J, but we bet you've never tried PB&S, peanut butter and s'mores, that is! This delicious dip is perfect for dunking with cookies, crackers, pretzels, and fruit.

Servings: 4

Total Time: 5mins

Ingredients:

- ¼ cup semi-skim milk
- ¼ cup smooth peanut butter
- 1 tbsp cocoa powder
- 1 cup whip topping
- ¼ cup mini mallows
- 6 graham crackers (broken into small pieces)
- Cookies, crackers, pretzels, fruit (for dipping)

Directions:

1. Whisk together the milk, peanut butter, and cocoa powder. Fold in the whip topping until incorporated.

2. Sprinkle with mini mallows and graham crackers.

3. Serve straight away with your favorite snacks for dipping.

Peanut Butter and Apple S'mores Pizza

A delicious dessert pizza topped with all the good stuff! Apples, peanut butter, mallows, chocolate, and graham crackers are a heavenly combination the family will go nuts for!

Servings: 4

Total Time: 30mins

Ingredients:

- Nonstick spray
- 14 ounces refrigerated readymade pizza dough.
- 1 cup smooth peanut butter (warmed)
- ½ cup graham crackers (broken into small pieces)
- 3 large granny smith apples (sliced thinly)
- 2 cups mini mallows
- ½ cup milk choc chips
- ¼ cup smooth peanut butter (warmed until runny)

Directions:

1. Preheat main oven to 350 degrees F and coat a pizza pan with nonstick spray.

2. Roll out the prepared dough into an even disc shape and place on the pan.

3. Spread the one cup of peanut butter onto the dough evenly.

4. Scatter with the crackers and arrange the apple slices neatly on top. Sprinkle with the mini mallows and choc chips.

5. Place in the oven and bake for just under 20minutes, allow to cool a little before slicing and serving drizzled with more warm peanut butter.

Perfect Pudding

Perfect for those busy days when you want delicious dessert but simply don't have the time to hang around in front of the stove. Whip up this perfect pudding at lunchtime and chill, to enjoy a delicious dessert by dinnertime.

Servings: 6

Total Time: 5hours 10mins

Ingredients:

- 1 (3½ ounce) box chocolate pudding mix
- 1 cup marshmallow crème
- 8 ounces whip topping
- 12 graham cracker squares (crumbled)
- Hot fudge sauce (warm, for serving)

Directions:

1. Prepare the chocolate pudding according to box instructions and set to one side for a moment.

2. Fold together the marshmallow crème and whip topping until combined, making sure not to overmix.

3. Fold the crumbled graham crackers and chocolate pudding into the whip topping mixture until only just combined, it does not matter if the mixture looks streaky.

4. Chill for 4-5 hours.

5. When ready to serve, spoon into bowl and drizzle with fudge sauce.

Raspberry and Apricot S'mores

Sweet apricot jam perfectly complements tart raspberries in an almond and mallow s'more, which is also a lighter alternative to the classic!

Servings: 1

Total Time: 10mins

Ingredients:

- 1 large marshmallow
- 2 almond thins
- ½ tsp apricot jam
- 4 fresh raspberries

Directions:

1. Toast the marshmallows over an open flame or fire.

2. Spread the jam on one almond thin, top with a toasted marshmallow followed by the raspberries.

3. Add the remaining almond thin to make a sandwich.

Rose Mallow and Vanilla Wafer, White Chocolate S'mores

Not only do these s'mores tasty good but they are pretty too, which makes them the ideal sweet treat for a buffet or party table!

Servings: 6

Total Time: 10mins

Ingredients:

- 12 vanilla wafers
- ½ (13½ ounce) bar white chocolate (cut into squares)
- 6 rose-flavored marshmallows (cut into ½-¾" cubes)

Directions:

1. Arrange 6 vanilla wafers, round side facing down onto a cookie sheet. Leave approximately 1" between each wafer.

2. On the top of the wafers, the flat side, evenly divide and place the cubes of white chocolate on top of the 6 wafers, followed by the marshmallows.

3. Carefully place the baking sheet in the oven and bake for 2½ minutes, or until the mallows are puffy and golden on the edges. Depending on the size of the mallows you may need to increase the time to 3 minutes.

4. Take the cookie sheet out of the oven and gently transfer the s'mores to a plate.

5. Place the top 6 wafers on the s'mores, flat side facing downwards, and gently press to secure.

Simple S'mores Ice Cream

The whole family will be asking for more of this indulgent homemade ice cream.

Servings: 2quarts

Total Time: 3hours 30mins

Ingredients:

- 1½ cups whipping cream
- 2 cups whole milk
- 1 tsp vanilla essence
- Pinch of salt
- 1½ cups granulated sugar
- 12 large marshmallows
- 6 whole graham cracker squares (crumbled)
- 1 (1 pound) chocolate bar (broken into pieces)

Directions:

1. In a bowl, combine the cream, milk, vanilla, salt, and sugar.

2. Pour the mixture into an ice cream churner and process according to the ice cream maker's instructions.

3. Meanwhile, arrange the marshmallows on a cookie sheet and grill, taking care not to burn the mallows, for approximately 2-3 minutes. Remove and set aside to cool.

4. When the ice cream has almost finished churning add the crumbled crackers along with the pieces of broken chocolate.

5. Tear the mallows apart and add to the ice cream before continuing to churn until the ice cream is ready.

6. Serve at once as soft serve or for more set ice cream, transfer to an airtight container and put in the freezer, overnight.

S'mores Bark

A tasty, no-bake candy treat that the kids can get involved with making. It would also make a great hostess gift!

Servings: 6

Total Time: 2hours 10mins

Ingredients:

- 2 cups vanilla-flavor yogurt
- 1 tbsp honey
- 1 tbsp cocoa powder
- ½ cup mini mallows
- ¾ cup graham cracker crumbs
- ½ cup milk choc chips

Directions:

1. Cover a cookie sheet with parchment.

2. Add half of the yogurt to a small bowl along with the honey and cocoa powder. Stir to combine.

3. Spread the other half of the yogurt onto the cookie sheet in an even ⅛" thick layer.

4. Drop spoonfuls of the chocolate yogurt on top and swirl the two yogurts together using a toothpick.

5. Sprinkle with mallows, cracker crumbs, and milk choc chips.

6. Freeze for a couple of hours until set, break into shards and enjoy.

S'mores Breakfast Oatmeal

You will have no trouble waking the family up when you serve this sweet and satisfying breakfast oatmeal.

Servings: 1

Total Time: 6mins

Ingredients:

- ½ cup old-fashioned oats
- 1 cup water
- 1 tbsp brown sugar
- ½ tbsp graham cracker crumbs
- ¼ cup mini mallows
- 2 tbsp mini semisweet choc chips

Directions:

1. In a microwave-safe bowl, combine the oats with the water and microwave for 3-4 minutes. Set to one side for a couple of minutes to allow the oatmeal to set.

2. Transfer the oatmeal to a bowl and add the brown sugar and cracker crumbs, stir to combine.

3. Add the mini mallows and choc chips and stir.

4. Enjoy.

S'mores Cheesecake

A make in advance cheesecake is an easy way to cater for a special occasion or get-together.

Servings: 16

Total Time: 12hours

Ingredients:

- 2 cups graham cracker crumbs
- ¼ cup sugar
- 6 tbsp butter (melted)
- 11½ ounces milk choc chips
- 1 (12 ounce) can evaporated milk (divided)
- 1½ pounds full-fat cream cheese (at room temperature)
- 7 ounces marshmallow crème
- 2 tbsp cornstarch
- 1 tsp vanilla essence
- 3 large eggs (lightly beaten)
- 2½ cups mini mallows

Directions:

1. Preheat the main oven to 325 degrees F.

2. In a bowl, combine the crumbed crackers with the sugar and stir in the butter.

3. Press the mixture into the base and 1" up the sides of a lightly greased 9" springform pan.

4. Put the baking pan on a baking sheet and bake in the preheated oven for 10 minutes.

5. Remove from the oven and allow to cool on a wire baking rack.

6. In the top of a double boiler, melt the choc chips along with ¾ cup of evaporated milk, stirring continually until smooth.

7. Pour the chocolate mixture into the now cooled crust and place in the freezer for 20 minutes to set.

8. In a mixing bowl, beat the cream cheese until silky.

9. Beat in the marshmallow fluff followed by the cornstarch, vanilla essence and remaining evaporated milk.

10. Add the lightly beaten eggs and beat until combined.

11. Pour the mixture over the chocolate and return the pan to the baking sheet.

12. Bake in the oven for 1-1¼ hours, until the middle is virtually set.

13. Scatter with mini marshmallows and bake for an additional 6-8 minutes, until the mallows are lightly browned.

14. Set aside to cool on a wire baking rack for 10 minutes.

15. Using a knife carefully loosen the cheesecake from the sides of the pan and set aside to cool for an additional 60 minutes.

16. Transfer to the fridge to chill, overnight. When cooled cover with a cloth.

17. Remove the rim from the springform pan and serve.

S'mores Fudge

Once friends and family sample this heavenly fudge they'll be begging for s'more!

Servings: 10-12

Total Time: 2hours 15mins

Ingredients:

- Nonstick spray
- 1 cup milk choc chips
- ½ cup chocolate hazelnut spread
- 1 (8 ounce) tub milk chocolate frosting
- ½ cup mini mallows
- ½ cup brown sugar graham square cereal

Directions:

1. Line a small baking dish with kitchen foil and coat with nonstick spray. Set to one side.

2. Melt together the choc chips, and chocolate spread using a microwave and stir very well.

3. Fold in the frosting until combined. Pop back in the microwave for 30-35 more seconds. Stir again.

4. Fold in the mallows and cereal.

5. Spoon the mixture into the dish, smoothing the surface.

6. Chill for a couple of hours until set, before slicing into squares and enjoying.

S'mores Hand Pies

Sticky marshmallow and melting chocolate filling are enveloped in golden buttery pastry for a delicious snack that will have you going back for s'more!

Servings: 10

Total Time: 35mins

Ingredients:

Pastry:

- ¼ cup granulated sugar
- ½ cup graham crackers crumbs
- 14 ounces readymade chilled pie crust dough
- 3 tbsp salted butter (melted)

Filling:

- 1 ounce full-fat cream cheese (at room temperature)
- ½ cup marshmallow crème
- 2 tbsp granulated sugar
- ½ cup milk choc chips

Directions:

1. Preheat the main oven to 425 degrees F. Cover a baking sheet with parchment.

2. First, make the pie crust. Combine the sugar and cracker crumbs on a plate.

3. Roll the chilled dough into a large even sheet and using a 3" cookie cutter, cut 20 rounds from the dough, re-rolling as necessary.

4. Brush each dough round with butter on both sides and dip into the cracker crumbs to coat.

5. Place 10 of the coated discs on the baking sheet.

6. Next, make the filling. Add the cream cheese, marshmallow crème, and sugar in a bowl and stir until combined. Fold in the choc chips.

7. Place 1 tbsp of filling onto each of the 10 dough discs on the baking sheet and top with remaining 10 dough discs to form 10 pies.

8. Press together all of the edges to seal.

9. Place in the oven and bake for approximately 10 minutes until golden. Allow to cool for 10-12 minutes before serving.

S'mores Hand Pies

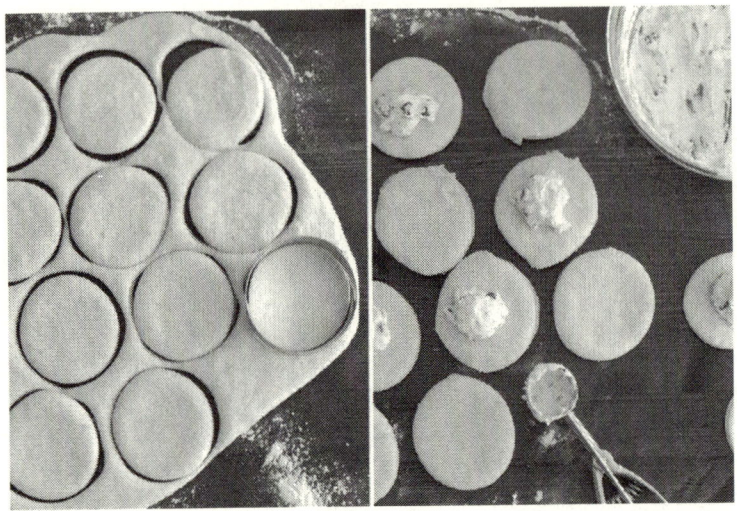

Sticky marshmallow and melting chocolate filling are enveloped in golden buttery pastry for a delicious snack that will have you going back for s'more!

Servings: 10

Total Time: 35mins

Ingredients:

Pastry:

- ¼ cup granulated sugar
- ½ cup graham crackers crumbs
- 14 ounces readymade chilled pie crust dough
- 3 tbsp salted butter (melted)

Filling:

- 1 ounce full-fat cream cheese (at room temperature)
- ½ cup marshmallow crème
- 2 tbsp granulated sugar
- ½ cup milk choc chips

Directions:

1. Preheat the main oven to 425 degrees F. Cover a baking sheet with parchment.

2. First, make the pie crust. Combine the sugar and cracker crumbs on a plate.

3. Roll the chilled dough into a large even sheet and using a 3" cookie cutter, cut 20 rounds from the dough, re-rolling as necessary.

4. Brush each dough round with butter on both sides and dip into the cracker crumbs to coat.

5. Place 10 of the coated discs on the baking sheet.

6. Next, make the filling. Add the cream cheese, marshmallow crème, and sugar in a bowl and stir until combined. Fold in the choc chips.

7. Place 1 tbsp of filling onto each of the 10 dough discs on the baking sheet and top with remaining 10 dough discs to form 10 pies.

8. Press together all of the edges to seal.

9. Place in the oven and bake for approximately 10 minutes until golden. Allow to cool for 10-12 minutes before serving.

S'mores on a Stick

This recipe is perfect and ideal for any child's party. It's colorful, fun and easy to make.

Servings: 24

Total Time: 2hours 10mins

Ingredients:

- 1 (14 ounces) can sweetened condensed milk (divided)
- 1 cup mini mallows
- 1½ cups semisweet choc chips (divided)
- 24 whole graham crackers (snapped in half)
- Rainbow sprinkles

Directions:

1. In a microwave-safe bowl, microwave on high, ⅔ cup of condensed milk for 90 seconds. Add the mallows along with 1 cup of choc chips and stir until lump-free.

2. Using a tablespoon drop the mixture onto, and evenly spread on 24 of the cracker halves.

3. Top with the remaining 24 halves and firmly but gently press down to make a sandwich.

4. In a microwave-safe bowl, microwave the remaining milk for 90 seconds. Add the remaining chocolate chips and stir thoroughly until silky smooth.

5. Drizzle the mixture over the cookies, decorate with assorted sprinkles and set aside for 2 hours.

6. After 2 hours has elapsed, insert a popsicle stick into the middle of each one.

S'mores Stuffed French Toast

We can't think of a better way to start the day than with golden French toast coated in graham cracker crumbs and layered with ooey gooey mallows and melting milk chocolate; all finished off with a generous drizzle of hot fudge sauce!

Servings: 2

Total Time: 20mins

Ingredients:

- 2 eggs (lightly beaten)
- ⅔ cup milk
- ¼ tsp table salt
- 1 tsp pure vanilla essence
- 1 cup graham crackers crumbs
- 3 slices thick-cut French bread
- Butter
- 6-8 large marshmallows (halved)
- 3 ounces milk chocolate chunks
- Hot fudge sauce (warm, for topping)

Directions:

1. Add the beaten eggs, milk, table salt, and vanilla in a shallow dish and whisk to combine.

2. Tip the graham crackers crumbs onto a plate.

3. Dip each slice of bread first into the milk mixture and then into the cracker crumbs to coat.

4. Melt a dab of butter in a large skillet over moderate heat and fry each slice of bread on both sides until golden and crisp.

5. Arrange one piece of toast on your serving plate and top with the marshmallows. Arrange the second piece of toast on top and place the chocolate chunks on the toast.

6. Finish by placing the second piece of toast over the chocolate chunks.

7. Drizzle generously with warmed fudge sauce. Enjoy!

S'mores Sushi

A super easy-to-make and tasty treat that your little ones will love. Why not enjoy with chopsticks for a fun and yummy snack!

Servings: 12

Total Time: 2hours 20mins

Ingredients:

- Nonstick spray
- ¼ cup salted butter
- 10 ounces mini mallows
- 5 cups crispy rice cereal
- 2 cups marshmallow crème
- 1 cup graham crackers (any brand, crushed)
- 1 cup semisweet choc chips (melted)
- 1 cup milk choc chips (melted)

Directions:

1. Line a baking sheet with a wax paper and coat with nonstick spray.

2. In a saucepan over low heat, melt the salted butter. Add the mallows and cook, while stirring, until the mallows melt and combine with the butter.

3. Remove from the heat and add the crispy rice cereal. Using a rubber spatula, carefully stir until completely combined.

4. Press the sticky cereal mixture onto the baking sheet, into a thin and compact rectangle-shape.

5. Spread the marshmallow crème evenly on top of the rectangle.

6. Sprinkle over the crushed crackers.

7. Carefully and gently, so as not to move the crackers, pour and spread the melted semisweet chocolate evenly on top.

8. Roll the rectangle up (from the wide edge) and cut into ¾" slices.

9. Cover a second baking sheet with a wax paper.

10. Carefully dip each piece of 'sushi' halfway into the melted milk chocolate to coat.

11. Arrange the dipped 'sushi' on the second cookie sheet.

12. Chill for a couple of hours until firm before enjoying (with or without chopsticks)!

S'mores Toffee

Toffee making doesn't need to be difficult. In fact, you can whip up a batch of this s'mores-flavored toffee in less time than it takes to go to the candy shop!

Servings: 16-20 servings

Total Time: 30mins

Ingredients:

- Graham crackers
- ½ cup best butter
- 1 cup packed brown sugar
- 1 (12 ounce) bag semisweet choc chips
- 1 (16 ounce) bag mini mallows

Directions:

1. Preheat the main oven to 350 degrees F.

2. Arrange a sufficient number of graham crackers to cover a 13x9" cookie sheet.

3. Over moderate heat, in a pan, combine the butter with the brown sugar, continually stirring. When the mixture comes to boil, slowly pour the butter mixture over the graham crackers and using a spatula spread as evenly as is possible.

4. Bake in the preheated oven for a few minutes.

5. Remove the cookie sheet from the oven and sprinkle with the choc chips. Allow 1-2 minutes for the chocolate to melt and then smooth out, using a spatula.

6. Scatter the mini mallows evenly over the top and return to the oven for 2-3 minutes, until toasted. Take great care not to burn the marshmallows.

7. Set the toffee aside to cool and set before breaking into bite-sized pieces. You can speed this process up by chilling in the fridge.

Strawberry Skillet S'mores

A simple, quick and delicious berry dessert the whole family can dig in to!

Servings: 8

Total Time: 10mins

Ingredients:

- 12 graham crackers
- 1 cup fresh strawberries (hulled, sliced)
- 1 cup mini mallows
- ½ cup dark choc chips

Directions:

1. Preheat your oven's broiler.

2. Arrange the graham crackers in the base of a skillet and arrange the sliced strawberries evenly on top.

3. Scatter with the mini mallows and choc chips.

4. Place under the broiler for 5-6 minutes until the chocolate melts, and mallows have turned golden.

5. Serve straight away.

Sunflower S'mores Dip

A sweet dip is perfect for a party or get-together with friends. Kids will love this dip too.

Servings: 12

Total Time: 20mins

Ingredients:

- ½ cup unsalted butter (softened)
- ½ cup creamy sunflower butter
- ½ cup brown sugar
- 8 ounces cream cheese (softened)
- 1 cup confectioner's sugar
- 1 tsp vanilla essence
- Pinch salt
- 1 cup chocolate candy bars (chopped, divided)
- 1 cup mini mallows (divided)
- Graham crackers (to serve)

Directions:

1. In the bowl of a hand or stand mixer, beat the butter along with the sunflower butter, and brown sugar until fluffy and light. Add the cream cheese and beat until lump free, scraping down the sides of the mixing bowl as needed.

2. Slowly and gradually beat in the confectioner's sugar, vanilla essence, and salt.

3. With a spatula, fold in approximately ¾ of a cup of chopped candy bar chocolate and ¾ cup of mini mallows.

4. Transfer to a bowl and sprinkle with the remaining chopped chocolate and mini mallows.

5. Transfer to the fridge to chill until ready to serve.

6. Serve with the graham crackers for dipping.

Tempting S'mores Truffles

Rich and indulgent chocolate ganache truffles with a surprise marshmallow center are rolled in graham crackers crumbs for a decadent pop in the mouth treat.

Servings: 12

Total Time: 3hours

Ingredients:

- ½ cup heavy cream
- 2 tbsp salted butter (melted)
- 2 cups milk choc chips
- 24 mini mallows
- 1 cup graham crackers (crumbs)

Directions:

1. Add the cream and salted butter to a saucepan over moderate heat and bring to a boil while whisking.

2. Take off the heat and whisk in the choc chips until they melt and the mixture is silky smooth.

3. Chill the mixture for 1-2 hours until solid.

4. Using a spoon to scoop the mixture and wet hands, roll into 24 equally-sized balls.

5. Insert a marshmallow into each ball. The best way to do this is first to make an indent in each truffle using your thumb, placing a mallow in the dent and then smoothing the truffle mixture around the mallow.

6. Chill for 10-12 minutes to firm up again.

7. Sprinkle the graham cracker crumbs onto a plate.

8. Roll the truffles in the crumbs to coat evenly and keep chilled until ready to enjoy.

The Original

Ooey gooey melting perfection from this classic and original s'mores recipe.

Servings: 8

Total Time: 25mins

Ingredients:

- 8 sheets honey graham crackers (halved crosswise into 2 squares)
- 1 (4¼ ounce) bar milk chocolate (snapped into 8 chunks)
- Pinch kosher salt
- 8 large marshmallows

Directions:

1. Heat your grill to moderately low heat.

2. Prepare 1 or 2 s'mores at a time; arrange 1 square of cracker on a sheet of aluminium foil and top with a chunk of chocolate and a pinch of salt. Place on the very edge of your grill, for 30 seconds to soften and warm the chocolate.

3. Transfer the cracker squares and pieces of the chocolate to the grilling area and working in batches, using a long fork or metal skewer, spear the marshmallows. Hold the mallows over the heat, approximately 2" above the grill grate. Toast, while occasionally turning, until the marshmallows become golden and puffed, this will take between 1-2 minutes.

4. Using the cracker square with the softened chocolate and a plain square place the toasted mallow on top of the chocolate and using the plain square, squash the melted mallow down, and carefully slide off the fork.

5. Eat and enjoy.

White Chocolate and Raspberry S'mores

A sophisticated twist on the classic s'more using fresh juicy raspberries and ultra creamy white chocolate.

Servings: 4

Total Time: 10mins

Ingredients:

- 4 whole graham crackers (snapped in half)
- 8 squares white chocolate
- 4 large marshmallows
- Small handful fresh raspberries

Directions:

1. On a microwave-safe plate, arrange the graham cracker halves.

2. Top 4 of the cracker halves with 1 square of white chocolate and a marshmallow. Top the remaining 4 with a square of chocolate.

3. Place in the microwave and cook for approximately 15-20 seconds, checking at 5-second intervals so as not to burn the white chocolate.

4. Top the 4 white chocolate-only topped graham crackers with a couple of raspberries and sandwich together with the chocolate and marshmallow-topped crackers to form 4 whole s'mores.

Drinks

Boozy S'mores Coffee

Set a little time aside for yourself and indulge in this ooey-gooey, chocolatey coffee.

Servings: 1

Total Time: 3mins

Ingredients:

- 6 ounces brewed coffee
- ½ ounce marshmallow flavored vodka
- ½ ounce chocolate flavored vodka
- Cream or milk (optional)
- ⅓ cup mini mallows
- 1 tbsp chocolate sauce
- ½ graham cracker (crumbled)

Directions:

1. In a coffee cup combine the coffee with the marshmallow and chocolate vodka.

2. Add the cream or milk, according to your preference.

3. Top with mini mallows.

4. Place the coffee cup on a baking sheet and under the broiler and with the oven door remaining open gently brown the mallows for 2-3 seconds,

5. Drizzle chocolate sauce over the toasted mallows and scatter with graham cracker crumbs.

Champagne and Vodka Cocktail

Chilled Champagne pairs with chocolate vodka for a sophisticated and grown-up way to savor the s'mores flavor.

Servings: 1

Total Time: 5mins

Ingredients:

- ¼ cup graham cracker crumbs
- 2 ounces chocolate flavor vodka
- 4 ounces Champagne (not brut, chilled)

Directions:

1. Add the cracker crumbs to a plate or dish.

2. Dip the rim of a Champagne flute in water.

3. Press the rim of the glass into the crumbs.

4. Pour the vodka into the flute and fill to the top will champagne.

5. Serve.

Chocolate and Mallow S'mores Margarita

Surprise your friends with a s'mores inspired Margarita, so good it's almost a dessert.

Servings: 4

Total Time: 7mins

Ingredients:

- Marshmallow crème (to rim)
- Chocolate sauce (to rim)
- 6 ounces silver tequila
- 4 ounces chocolate liqueur
- ½ cup chocolate syrup
- ⅓ cup cream
- Ice
- Mini mallows

Directions:

1. First, rim the glass with marshmallow crème and dip in chocolate sauce.

2. Combine the tequila, chocolate liqueur, syrup and cream in an ice-filled cocktail shaker.

3. Spear 3 mini mallows on a cocktail stick and rest across the rim of the glass.

4. Serve.

Flaming S'mores Vodka and Rum Cocktail

Enjoy the flavor and aroma of roasting mallows on an open fire without having to leave the comfort of home.

Servings: 1

Total Time: 7mins

Ingredients:

- 4 graham crackers (finely crushed)
- 1 (28g) sachet hot chocolate
- 2 tbsp marshmallow crème or fluff
- 3 mini mallows
- Ice
- 2 ounces marshmallow vodka
- 2 ounces chocolate liqueur
- 1 ounce heavy cream
- 1 ounce high-alcohol white rum

Directions:

1. Combine the finely crushed crackers with the sachet of hot chocolate.

2. Rim a martini glass by dipping first, in the marshmallow creme/fluff and second in the cracker-chocolate mixture.

3. Spear 3 mini mallows on a cocktail stick and rest on the side of the martini glass.

4. Fill a shaker with ice, and add the marshmallow vodka, chocolate liqueur, and heavy cream. Shake it all about and strain into the martini glass.

5. Gently pour the white rum onto the surface of the drink. You can do this by placing a teaspoon upside down in the martini glass. Place the spoon so that it touches the side of the glass and carefully pour the alcohol into the glass, making sure it remains in contact with the side of the glass and slowly dribble over the teaspoon.

6. Light the alcohol with a crème brulee torch.

7. Toast the mallows on the flame and serve as soon as the alcohol has completely burned off.

Hot Chocolate with Mallows and Crumbs

What better hot, bedtime drink is there? Creamy, chocolatey and super indulgent.

Servings: 1

Total Time: 6mins

Ingredients:

- 1 cup unsweetened almond milk
- ¼ cup dark choc chips
- 1 tsp vanilla essence
- 1 tsp pure maple syrup
- 1 tbsp graham cracker crumbs
- Mini mallows
- Chocolate syrup (to drizzle)

Directions:

1. In a pan over moderate heat, heat the milk together with the chocolate chips and vanilla essence, continually whisking until the chocolate melts and the milk is steaming hot.

2. Drizzle the maple syrup onto a plate and rim the top of a coffee mug in the syrup. Add the cracker crumbs to another plate and roll the rim of the mug in the crumbs.

3. Pour the cocoa into the mug and sprinkle with mini mallows.

4. Scatter any remaining cracker crumbs on top and drizzle with syrup.

Irish Whiskey in the Jar

You will definitely want s'more of this decadent drink!

Servings: 1

Total Time: 10mins

Ingredients:

- Graham crackers (crushed)
- Mini mallows
- Chocolate sauce
- 3 large marshmallows
- 3 ounces Irish whiskey

Directions:

1. Add the crushed crackers to the bottom of a mason jar.

2. Add a layer of mini mallows, followed by a layer of chocolate sauce (amounts to suit your taste).

3. Top with the large mallows.

4. Drizzle with Irish whiskey.

5. Using a crème brulee torch, brown the large mallows.

Oh So Sweet S'mores Smoothie

The perfect mid-morning snack or supper time treat.

Servings: 1

Total Time: 5mins

Ingredients:

- 1 ripe banana (peeled)
- ½ cup sweetened almond milk
- 1 graham cracker sheet
- 2 tbsp marshmallow crème
- 2 tsp cocoa powder
- 5-6 ice cubes
- Mini choc chips (to serve)
- ½ graham cracker sheet (crushed)

Directions:

1. In the jug of a food blender, combine the banana with the milk, 1 cracker sheet, marshmallow crème, cocoa powder, and ice cubes. Process for 60 seconds until smooth.

2. Pour the smoothie into a mason jar.

3. Garnish with mini choc chips and sprinkle with crushed crackers.

4. Enjoy.

Party S'mores Jello Shots

These sweet and boozy jello shots are a real party pleaser.

Servings: 12

Total Time: 3hours 10mins

Ingredients:

- 1 cup water
- 1 (1 ounce) sachet hot chocolate mix
- 5 tsp powdered gelatin
- 1 cup Irish cream whiskey
- 12 jumbo marshmallows
- ⅓ cup choc chips (melted)
- 5 graham crackers (crushed)

Directions:

1. In a small pan, combine the water with the chocolate mix and gelatin. Set to one side for 60 seconds.

2. Increase the heat to moderate and bring to boil while occasionally whisking, until the ingredients are completely dissolved.

3. Turn the heat off and whisk in the Irish cream. Set to one side to cool.

4. Using a teaspoon, carefully scoop out the middle of the marshmallows to make a shot glass. Pierce with a skewer and lightly toast.

5. Dip the hollowed out part of the mallows into the melted chocolate and then into the crushed crackers.

6. Fill the 'shots' with the cooled cocoa mixture and transfer to the fridge until set, for approximately 3 hours.

7. Serve.

S'morestini

This martini is well worth the effort and has to be the best Over-21 way to enjoy the comforting flavor of s'mores.

Servings: 1

Total Time: 10mins (plus 7 days infusing)

Ingredients:

For Vodka:

- 1 (750ml) bottle of vanilla vodka
- 10 sticks cinnamon

Martini:

- Marshmallow crème (to rim)
- Graham cracker crumbs (to rim)
- Cocoa powder (to rim)
- 1 ounce honey scotch
- 1 ounce chocolate liqueur
- Splash of chocolate bitters
- Ice
- 2 ounces heavy cream
- 1 tsp organic honey
- Toasted marshmallows (to serve)

Directions:

1. First, prepare the cinnamon and vanilla flavor vodka. Pour the vodka into a mason jar. Add the sticks of cinnamon and cover. Transfer to a cool and dark environment for 7 days. You will need to shake the jar every day. Strain the liquid and discard the sticks of cinnamon.

2. When you are ready to make the martini, first rim the glass. Rim first with marshmallow crème.

3. On a plate combine the graham crumbs with the cocoa powder, stir to combine. Dip the rim of the glass in the crumb mixture. Lightly toast the marshmallow rim using a crème brulee torch.

4. Add 1 ounce of the cinnamon and vanilla flavored vodka along with the honey scotch, chocolate liqueur, and bitters to an ice-filled cocktail shaker. Shake it all about until it froths.

5. Strain the cocktail into the rimmed glasses.

6. Rinse the cocktail shaker and fill with ice.

7. Add the heavy cream followed by the honey to the shaker and with no ice, shake it all about until the liquid is a thick consistency.

8. Spoon the mixture over the top of the cocktail and garnish with a toasted marshmallow.

S'mores Shake

Your little ones will love this ice cream shake almost as much as you!

Servings: 4

Total Time: 15mins

Ingredients:

- 4 large marshmallows
- 3 cups vanilla ice cream
- ½ cup chocolate spread or syrup
- ½ cup marshmallow crème
- 3 full graham cracker sheets
- ½ cup chocolate bars (chopped)
- 4 tbsp mini chocolate chips
- 4 tbsp mini marshmallows
- 4 tbsp graham cracker crumbs

Directions:

1. First, toast the marshmallows. Set to one side.

2. In a blender or mixer combine the ice cream, with the chocolate spread, marshmallow crème, cracker sheets and chopped chocolate.

3. Divide the mixture between 4 glasses and top with mini choc chips, mini mallows, cracker crumbs.

4. Serve each shake with 1 large toasted marshmallow.

About the author

Gordon Rock is the author for hundreds of cookbooks on delicious meals that the 'average Joe' can attempt at home. Including, but definitely not limited to, the Amazon Prime bestseller "Smoking Meat: The Essential Guide to Real Barbecue".

Rock is also known for other well-known titles such as "Making Fresh Pasta", "Hot Sauce", "The Paleo Chocolate Lovers" and "Vegan Tacos", just to name a few.

Rock has been nominated for various awards and has recently been offered a 'Question & Answers' column in Food and Wine Magazine that will give him a greater medium to respond to all the queries readers may have after attempting his recipes. He has also been honored by the Institution of Culinary Excellence for his outstanding recipes.

Gordon Rock grew up in the outskirts of Los Angeles in California, where he graduated from the Culinary Institute of America with honors. He still resides there along with his wife and three kids. He operates a non - profit organization for aspiring cooks who are unable to finance their culinary education and spends practically all his spare time either in the kitchen or around his desk writing.

Author's Afterthoughts

Thanks ever so much to each of my cherished readers for investing the time to read this book!

I know you could have picked from many other books but you chose this one. So a big thanks for downloading this book and reading all the way to the end.

If you enjoyed this book or received value from it, I'd like to ask you for a favor. Please take a few minutes to post an honest and heartfelt review on Amazon.com. Your support does make a difference and helps to benefit other people.

Thanks for your Reviews!

Gordon Rock

Made in the USA
Lexington, KY
29 December 2018